Empowering Voices: Language Acquisition for Everyone, Including the Deaf Community

Igor Petrov

1

Copyright © [2023]

Author: Igor Petrov

Title: Empowering Voices: Language Acquisition for Everyone, Including the Deaf Community

This book is a product of [Publisher's Igor Petrov]

ISBN:

TABLE OF CONTENTS

Chapter 1: Introduction to Language Acquisition for Individuals with Hearing Impairments

Understanding Hearing Impairments

Hearing impairments, also known as hearing loss or deafness, are conditions that affect a person's ability to hear or understand sounds. It is important for everyone, including those in the field of language acquisition, to have a comprehensive understanding of hearing impairments and their impact on individuals' lives. This subchapter aims to provide a broad overview of hearing impairments, their causes, and various communication methods used by the deaf community.

Hearing impairments can be categorized into different types based on their severity and the affected part of the auditory system. Conductive hearing loss occurs when there is a problem in the outer or middle ear, which hinders sound transmission to the inner ear. Sensorineural hearing loss, on the other hand, results from damage to the inner ear or auditory nerve, making it difficult to perceive sound properly. Mixed hearing loss combines elements of both conductive and sensorineural hearing loss.

There are several factors that contribute to hearing impairments, including genetics, infections, exposure to loud noises, trauma, and certain medications. It is crucial to understand that hearing impairments are not solely physical conditions but can also have a significant impact on a person's linguistic and cognitive development. This is particularly relevant to language acquisition, as hearing impairments can affect a person's ability to acquire spoken language naturally.

To address the communication needs of individuals with hearing impairments, various methods have been developed. Sign language, such as American Sign Language (ASL), is a visual-gestural language that uses handshapes, facial expressions, and body movements to convey meaning. Sign language is a vibrant and rich language with its own grammar and syntax, and it is important to recognize it as a legitimate language in its own right.

Other communication methods include lip-reading, which involves visually interpreting the movement of the speaker's lips, and the use of assistive devices like hearing aids and cochlear implants. These devices amplify sound or directly stimulate the auditory nerve to enhance hearing.

Understanding hearing impairments is crucial for language acquisition professionals, as it allows them to develop inclusive and effective strategies to support individuals with hearing impairments in their language development journey. By recognizing the diversity within the deaf community and embracing various communication methods, we can empower individuals with hearing impairments to fully participate in language acquisition and foster a more inclusive society.

In conclusion, this subchapter provided an overview of hearing impairments, their causes, and the various communication methods used by the deaf community. It highlighted the importance of understanding hearing impairments in the field of language acquisition to ensure inclusive language development for individuals with hearing impairments. By embracing diverse communication methods and recognizing the linguistic richness of sign language, we can empower individuals with hearing impairments to acquire language and participate fully in society.

Importance of Language Acquisition for the Deaf Community

The Importance of Language Acquisition for the Deaf Community

Language acquisition is a fundamental aspect of human development, allowing us to communicate, express our thoughts and emotions, and connect with others. While spoken language is the most common form of communication, it is essential to recognize the unique needs and experiences of the deaf community in relation to language acquisition.

For individuals in the deaf community, language acquisition takes a different path. Deaf individuals often rely on sign languages, such as American Sign Language (ASL), to communicate effectively. These languages, just like spoken languages, have their grammar, vocabulary, and syntax, enabling deaf individuals to express themselves fully.

The ability to acquire and use sign language is crucial for the deaf community as it provides them with a means of communication and access to information. Without language acquisition, deaf individuals may experience isolation, limited education opportunities, and a decreased ability to participate in society.

Language acquisition is especially vital during early childhood. Research has shown that early exposure to sign language is essential for optimal language development and cognitive growth in deaf children. Just as hearing children benefit from early exposure to spoken language, deaf children thrive when they are exposed to sign language from an early age.

Furthermore, language acquisition for the deaf community goes beyond the acquisition of sign languages. Many deaf individuals also learn to read and write in their local written language, such as English or Spanish. This empowers them to navigate educational and professional settings where written communication is essential.

In our society, where spoken language dominates, it is crucial for everyone to recognize and appreciate the importance of language acquisition for the deaf community. By embracing and supporting sign languages, we promote inclusivity and create a more accessible environment for deaf individuals.

Language acquisition can be facilitated through educational programs that emphasize the teaching of sign languages, promote bilingualism, and encourage cultural understanding. By providing these resources, we empower the deaf community to fully participate in society, pursue educational and career opportunities, and express their unique voices.

In conclusion, language acquisition is of utmost importance for the deaf community. It opens doors to communication, education, and social integration. By recognizing and supporting the unique linguistic needs of the deaf community, we can create a more inclusive and empowering society for everyone.

Chapter 2: Historical Perspectives on Language Acquisition for the Deaf

Early Approaches to Deaf Education

In the journey towards understanding and empowering the deaf community, it is crucial to explore the early approaches to deaf education. These early methods laid the foundation for the advancements we see today in language acquisition for the deaf community. Understanding the historical context of how deaf education evolved is essential to appreciate the progress made and the challenges that still lie ahead.

One of the earliest approaches to deaf education was the oralism approach, which focused on teaching deaf individuals to speak and lip-read. This approach emerged in the 18th century and gained popularity throughout the 19th century. Advocates of oralism believed that deaf individuals could integrate into society more effectively if they could communicate orally, rather than relying on sign language. This approach often involved speech training and lip-reading instruction, with limited emphasis on sign language.

Another early approach to deaf education was the manualism approach. This approach recognized the importance of sign language as a natural language for the deaf community. Manualism emphasized the use of sign language as the primary mode of communication and aimed to develop deaf individuals' literacy skills in their native sign language. This approach gained momentum in the late 19th century and early 20th century.

The debate between oralism and manualism created a divide within the deaf education community, with each approach having its proponents and critics. However, it is important to note that both approaches played significant roles in shaping the field of deaf education and language acquisition.

Over time, a more balanced approach called Total Communication emerged, which aimed to utilize all available communication methods, including sign language, speech, lip-reading, and written language. This approach recognized the importance of individualized education plans and tailoring instruction to suit each deaf individual's needs.

Today, the field of deaf education continues to evolve, with a greater emphasis on inclusive practices and recognizing the diversity within the deaf community. Sign language is now recognized as a legitimate language, and bilingual-bicultural approaches are gaining recognition, encouraging the use of sign language alongside spoken language.

As we continue to empower voices within the deaf community, it is important to acknowledge the early approaches to deaf education that paved the way for the progress we see today. By understanding the historical context, we can appreciate the challenges faced by the deaf community and work towards creating inclusive and effective language acquisition strategies for everyone.

Sign Language and the Emergence of Deaf Culture

Language is the cornerstone of human communication, enabling us to express our thoughts, emotions, and ideas. While spoken language is the most common form of communication, it is essential to acknowledge the existence and significance of sign language. Sign language is a visual-gestural mode of communication used predominantly by individuals who are Deaf or hard of hearing.

Contrary to popular belief, sign languages are not universal. Just as spoken languages differ across countries and regions, sign languages also vary worldwide. For instance, American Sign Language (ASL) is distinct from British Sign Language (BSL) or Australian Sign Language (Auslan). These sign languages have their own lexicons, syntax, and grammar rules.

The emergence of sign language was a pivotal moment for the Deaf community. It provided a means of communication that allowed Deaf individuals to engage fully in society, express themselves, and connect with others who shared similar experiences. Through sign language, the Deaf community developed a unique culture that celebrates their language and identity.

Deaf culture encompasses a rich heritage, shared experiences, and a strong sense of community among Deaf individuals. It includes traditions, art, literature, social norms, and values that are distinct to the Deaf community. One of the central aspects of Deaf culture is the use of sign language as the primary mode of communication.

The recognition and acceptance of sign language as a legitimate language has been a significant milestone in the empowerment of the

Deaf community. It has allowed Deaf individuals to access education, employment, and various social opportunities on an equal footing with their hearing counterparts.

Language acquisition for everyone, including the Deaf community, is a crucial aspect of fostering inclusivity and breaking down barriers. By understanding and appreciating sign language, we can bridge the communication gap that often exists between the hearing and Deaf communities. It promotes empathy, understanding, and respect for diverse forms of communication.

In conclusion, sign language and the emergence of Deaf culture have had a profound impact on the lives of Deaf individuals. It has given them a voice, a means to express themselves, and a sense of belonging within a community that shares their experiences. Recognizing the importance of sign language and its role in language acquisition for everyone is an essential step towards creating a more inclusive and accessible society for all.

Chapter 3: The Role of Sign Language in Language Acquisition

Sign Language as a Natural Language

In the world of language acquisition, there is a prevailing misconception that only spoken languages are considered "natural" languages. However, this notion is far from the truth. Sign language, used primarily by the deaf community, is indeed a natural language in every sense of the term. In this subchapter, we will explore the fascinating aspects of sign language and its significance in empowering voices within the deaf community and beyond.

Sign language is not merely a collection of hand gestures; it is a complete linguistic system with its own grammar, syntax, and vocabulary. Just like spoken languages, sign languages have regional and cultural variations, further emphasizing their status as natural languages. For instance, American Sign Language (ASL) differs significantly from British Sign Language (BSL), despite both being used by English-speaking communities.

One of the most remarkable aspects of sign language is its visual and spatial nature. Signers utilize their hands, facial expressions, and body movements to convey meaning, creating a rich and expressive mode of communication. This visual-spatial aspect makes sign language accessible not only to the deaf community but also to those with language difficulties or individuals from different linguistic backgrounds.

Contrary to popular belief, sign language has been used for centuries, with historical records dating back to ancient civilizations. It has evolved alongside spoken languages, with its own unique structure and rules. Research has shown that sign languages engage the same regions of the brain as spoken languages, further affirming their status as natural languages and debunking any notion of inferiority.

Sign language plays a crucial role in empowering voices within the deaf community. It provides a means of communication that allows deaf individuals to express their thoughts, emotions, and ideas on par with their hearing counterparts. By recognizing sign language as a natural language, we can break down communication barriers and promote inclusivity and equal opportunities for the deaf community.

Furthermore, understanding sign language as a natural language has broader implications for language acquisition as a whole. By acknowledging the validity and richness of sign languages, we can expand our understanding of linguistic diversity and challenge the dominant spoken language-centric perspective. This recognition can lead to more inclusive language education policies and practices, benefiting not only the deaf community but also individuals struggling with language acquisition.

In conclusion, sign language is undoubtedly a natural language, deserving of the same recognition and respect as any spoken language. Its visual-spatial nature, linguistic complexity, and historical significance make it an essential tool for empowering voices within the deaf community. By embracing sign language as a natural language, we can foster inclusivity, challenge linguistic biases, and create a more equitable society for everyone.

Types of Sign Language Systems

In the world of communication, sign languages play a vital role in bridging the gap between individuals who are deaf or hard of hearing and the rest of the population. Sign languages are visual-gestural languages, using a combination of hand movements, facial expressions, and body postures to convey meaning. However, not all sign languages are the same. This subchapter explores the different types of sign language systems that exist, highlighting their unique characteristics and significance in empowering language acquisition for everyone, including the deaf community.

1. American Sign Language (ASL): ASL is one of the most well-known sign languages used in North America. It has its own grammar structure and vocabulary, separate from English. ASL is recognized as a distinct language, with its own cultural nuances and regional variations.

2. British Sign Language (BSL): BSL is the sign language used in the United Kingdom. Similar to ASL, it has its own grammar and vocabulary. BSL is essential for individuals in the UK who are deaf or hard of hearing to communicate effectively with one another and with the hearing community.

3. International Sign (IS): International Sign is a sign language used as a lingua franca among deaf individuals from different countries. It serves as a means of communication at international events, such as conferences and sporting events, where participants may not share a common sign language. IS is created by combining elements from

various sign languages, making it more easily understood by a diverse group of signers.

4. Signed Exact English (SEE): SEE is a sign system that follows English grammar and vocabulary more closely. It is often used in educational settings to support language acquisition for deaf children. SEE aims to provide a visual representation of English, incorporating signs for each word, as well as the grammatical structure of the language.

5. Pidgin Sign Language (PSL): PSL is a simplified form of sign language that develops when individuals with different sign languages come together and need to communicate. PSL typically arises in situations where there is no shared language, such as in deaf communities with high linguistic diversity. It combines elements from different sign languages, resulting in a simplified and universal form of communication.

Understanding the various sign language systems is crucial for language acquisition for everyone, including the deaf community. By recognizing and respecting the diversity of sign languages, we can foster inclusive communication and empower individuals with different communication needs. Whether it is ASL, BSL, IS, SEE, or PSL, each sign language system plays a vital role in breaking barriers and connecting people across linguistic and cultural boundaries.

Chapter 4: Challenges and Strategies in Language Acquisition for the Deaf

Barriers to Language Acquisition

Language acquisition is a complex process that allows individuals to develop and express their thoughts, feelings, and ideas. However, there are various barriers that can hinder this process, making it challenging for individuals to acquire a new language effectively. In this subchapter, we will explore some of the common barriers to language acquisition and discuss strategies to overcome them.

One of the primary barriers to language acquisition is a lack of exposure to the target language. Language learning requires constant exposure and practice, but individuals may face limited opportunities to interact with native speakers or immerse themselves in the language. This can be particularly challenging for individuals living in non-English speaking countries or those who do not have access to language learning resources. To overcome this barrier, individuals can seek out language exchange programs, find native speakers to practice with, or utilize online resources and language learning platforms to enhance their exposure.

Another significant barrier is the fear of making mistakes and embarrassment. Many individuals are hesitant to speak a new language due to the fear of sounding incorrect or being judged. This fear can impede language acquisition as it hinders practice and engagement. To overcome this barrier, it is crucial to create a supportive and non-judgmental environment that encourages learners to take risks and embrace their mistakes. Language learners should understand that making errors is a natural part of the learning process and an opportunity for growth.

Cultural and social barriers can also impact language acquisition. Different cultures have unique communication styles, gestures, and norms, which can pose challenges for learners. Additionally, social barriers such as discrimination or exclusion can hinder language development, particularly for marginalized communities. It is essential to address these barriers by promoting cultural sensitivity, inclusivity, and providing resources that cater to diverse linguistic and cultural backgrounds.

Furthermore, individuals with hearing impairments face additional barriers in language acquisition. Traditional language learning methods primarily focus on auditory input, making it challenging for the deaf community to acquire spoken languages. However, with advancements in technology and the recognition of sign languages as legitimate languages, the barriers for the deaf community are gradually being dismantled. Incorporating visual cues, sign language instruction, and inclusive teaching methods can empower individuals from the deaf community to acquire language effectively.

In conclusion, language acquisition can be hindered by various barriers such as limited exposure, fear of making mistakes, cultural and social differences, and specific challenges faced by the deaf community. By understanding and addressing these barriers, we can create an inclusive and supportive environment that empowers individuals to acquire language effectively.

Language Acquisition in Different Age Groups

Language acquisition is a fascinating process that occurs naturally in humans, enabling us to communicate and connect with others. However, the age at which we begin acquiring language can have a significant impact on how we learn and use it. In this subchapter, we will explore the various age groups and their unique experiences in language acquisition.

Infancy is the critical period for language development. Babies are born with an innate ability to learn any language, absorbing sounds, intonations, and patterns effortlessly. They start by babbling and imitating the sounds they hear, gradually progressing to forming words and sentences. Infants thrive on interaction and exposure to language, so it is crucial for parents and caregivers to engage in conversation and provide a rich linguistic environment.

Toddlers and preschoolers continue to refine their language skills. They rapidly expand their vocabulary and begin to understand grammar rules. At this stage, language acquisition is heavily influenced by social interactions and exposure to diverse language models. Preschoolers benefit from interactive activities, such as storytelling and singing, to enhance their linguistic abilities further.

School-age children solidify their language skills and develop more complex language structures. They acquire new vocabulary through reading, writing, and engaging in conversations with peers and adults. Formal instruction plays a significant role in their language development, as it helps them understand grammar rules and refine their communication skills.

Teenagers experience language acquisition in a unique way. They not only focus on expanding their vocabulary but also develop their own identity through language. They may experiment with different linguistic styles and slang to fit in with their peer group. Additionally, teenagers who are learning a second language face the challenge of balancing their native language with the new language they are acquiring.

Adult language acquisition is a different process altogether. While adults can still learn new languages, they face certain challenges compared to children. Adults often rely on conscious learning strategies and may struggle with pronunciation due to their existing language habits. However, they bring their prior knowledge and life experiences, which can accelerate their language acquisition process.

Language acquisition is a lifelong journey that continues to evolve throughout our lives. Regardless of age, it is essential to create a nurturing and stimulating environment for language learning. By understanding the unique experiences and challenges faced by different age groups, we can empower individuals of all ages to acquire and master language skills, including those in the deaf community.

In conclusion, language acquisition varies across different age groups, with each stage presenting its own set of opportunities and challenges. By recognizing these differences and tailoring language acquisition strategies accordingly, we can ensure that everyone, including the deaf community, has access to effective language learning methods and the opportunity to participate fully in society.

Effective Strategies for Language Acquisition

Language acquisition is a fundamental skill that enables effective communication and connection with others. Whether you are a native speaker or learning a new language, there are various strategies that can enhance your language acquisition process. In this subchapter, we will explore some effective strategies for language acquisition that are beneficial for everyone, including the deaf community.

1. Immersion: One of the most effective ways to acquire a language is through immersion. Immerse yourself in environments where the language is spoken, such as traveling to a country where the language is prevalent or participating in language exchange programs. This allows you to interact with native speakers, practice your language skills, and gain a deeper understanding of the culture associated with the language.

2. Practice and Repetition: Consistent practice and repetition are key to language acquisition. Set aside dedicated time each day to practice listening, speaking, reading, and writing in the target language. Engage in conversations with native speakers, read books or articles in the language, and write essays or journal entries. By exposing yourself to the language regularly, you will improve your language skills over time.

3. Utilize Technology: In today's digital age, technology offers numerous resources for language acquisition. Utilize language learning apps, online courses, podcasts, and language exchange platforms to enhance your learning experience. These resources provide interactive exercises, audiovisual materials, and opportunities

for communication with native speakers, making language acquisition more accessible and engaging.

4. Cultural Immersion: Language and culture are intertwined, so immersing yourself in the culture associated with the language you are learning can greatly enhance your language acquisition. Explore the literature, music, films, and traditions of the culture to gain a deeper understanding of the language's nuances and context.

5. Seek Support: Language acquisition can be challenging, but seeking support from language tutors, teachers, or language communities can provide invaluable guidance and motivation. Join language learning groups, attend language exchange events, or find a language partner to practice and receive feedback on your language skills.

6. Be Patient and Persistent: Language acquisition takes time and effort, so it is crucial to be patient and persistent. Remember that making mistakes is a natural part of the learning process, and each mistake is an opportunity for improvement. Celebrate your progress, no matter how small, and stay committed to your language learning journey.

In conclusion, effective language acquisition strategies involve immersing yourself in the language, practicing regularly, utilizing technology, embracing the associated culture, seeking support, and maintaining patience and persistence. By implementing these strategies, you can empower your voice and enhance your language acquisition journey, regardless of your background or abilities.

Chapter 5: Technology and Language Acquisition for the Deaf Community

Assistive Listening Devices

In today's diverse world, effective communication is essential for everyone. Language acquisition plays a crucial role in connecting individuals and fostering meaningful interactions. However, it is important to recognize that language acquisition extends beyond the realm of spoken words. The deaf community, in particular, faces unique challenges in acquiring language and engaging in conversations. This subchapter aims to shed light on the significance of assistive listening devices in empowering voices within the deaf community and promoting inclusive language acquisition for everyone.

Assistive listening devices (ALDs) are technological tools designed to enhance sound perception and understanding for individuals with hearing impairments. These devices bridge the communication gap by amplifying sounds and reducing background noise, thus ensuring effective communication for individuals who rely on visual cues or assistive technologies to comprehend spoken language.

One of the most common ALDs is the hearing aid. These small, discreet devices are worn behind or inside the ear, amplifying sounds and making them clearer for individuals with varying degrees of hearing loss. Hearing aids are particularly beneficial for individuals with mild to moderate hearing impairments, allowing them to engage in conversations and participate actively in language acquisition.

Another essential ALD is the cochlear implant. This surgically implanted device bypasses damaged parts of the inner ear and stimulates the auditory nerve directly, enabling individuals with severe to profound hearing loss to perceive sound. Cochlear implants have revolutionized language acquisition for the deaf community, as they provide access to spoken language and enable individuals to communicate more effectively.

Additionally, assistive listening devices such as personal FM systems, loop systems, and captioning devices further enhance communication experiences for individuals with hearing impairments. Personal FM systems transmit sound directly from a speaker's microphone to an individual's hearing aid or cochlear implant, reducing background noise and improving speech intelligibility. Loop systems, on the other hand, use electromagnetic fields to transmit sound from a speaker directly to hearing aids, eliminating the need for a separate receiver. Captioning devices provide real-time captions for individuals who rely on visual cues or sign language, ensuring they can follow spoken content accurately.

By embracing assistive listening devices, we can promote inclusive language acquisition for everyone, including the deaf community. These devices empower individuals with hearing impairments by providing them with the tools necessary to engage in conversations, acquire language, and express themselves effectively. Let us strive towards a world where language acquisition is accessible to all, fostering connections, understanding, and inclusivity.

Cochlear Implants and Language Development

In recent years, cochlear implants have revolutionized the way we approach language acquisition for individuals with hearing impairments. This subchapter will delve into the impact of cochlear implants on language development, exploring how this technology has empowered not only the deaf community but also everyone involved in the realm of language acquisition.

Cochlear implants are electronic devices that provide a sense of sound to individuals with severe to profound hearing loss. By bypassing damaged parts of the ear, these implants directly stimulate the auditory nerve, allowing recipients to perceive sound. This breakthrough technology has opened up a world of possibilities for language acquisition among individuals who are deaf or hard of hearing.

For the deaf community, cochlear implants have offered a transformative solution, enabling them to access auditory information and engage in spoken language. While sign language remains a crucial form of communication within the deaf community, cochlear implants have facilitated the development of spoken language skills, creating new avenues for social integration and professional opportunities.

Moreover, cochlear implants have had a significant impact on language acquisition research and practice. Experts in the field have gained valuable insights into the process of acquiring spoken language, shedding light on the intricate relationship between auditory input and language development. This knowledge has not only benefited individuals with hearing impairments but has also influenced language acquisition strategies for the wider population.

Cochlear implants have proven particularly effective when implemented early in a child's life. Research has demonstrated that children who receive cochlear implants at a young age, before the critical period for language acquisition ends, can develop language skills on par with their hearing peers. This finding underscores the importance of early intervention and highlights the potential of cochlear implants in bridging the language gap between individuals with hearing impairments and the general population.

In conclusion, cochlear implants have transformed the landscape of language acquisition for individuals with hearing impairments. This subchapter has explored the impact of cochlear implants on language development within the deaf community, as well as their broader implications for language acquisition research and practice. By empowering voices and enabling spoken language skills, cochlear implants have not only changed the lives of individuals with hearing impairments but have also enriched our understanding of language acquisition for everyone.

Captioning and Subtitling for Language Acquisition

In today's diverse and interconnected world, language acquisition has become more important than ever. Whether it is for personal growth, professional development, or simply to communicate with others, the ability to acquire new languages opens up countless opportunities. However, it is crucial to acknowledge that language acquisition is not a one-size-fits-all process. Different individuals have different needs and preferences when it comes to learning languages, and it is essential to provide inclusive and accessible resources to cater to these diverse requirements.

Captioning and subtitling have emerged as valuable tools in the realm of language acquisition. Traditionally associated with making audiovisual content accessible to individuals with hearing impairments, captioning and subtitling have evolved to serve a broader purpose. They now play a significant role in language learning for everyone, including the deaf community.

Captioning refers to the process of displaying a text version of the audio elements in a video or audio recording. This allows individuals to read along with the spoken words, enhancing comprehension and retention. Subtitling, on the other hand, involves the translation of spoken words into written text, particularly when the language being spoken is different from the audience's native language. By providing translated subtitles, individuals can follow the dialogue and understand the content more effectively.

Captioning and subtitling have several benefits for language acquisition. Firstly, they provide visual reinforcement of spoken language, helping learners connect words with their written forms. This visual support aids in vocabulary acquisition and improves reading skills. Secondly, captioning and subtitling foster listening skills by allowing learners to associate spoken words with their corresponding written representations. This association helps individuals develop their auditory processing abilities, enabling them to comprehend spoken language more efficiently.

Moreover, captioning and subtitling promote language immersion, enabling learners to immerse themselves in the target language while watching movies, TV shows, or online videos. This immersive experience enhances language acquisition by exposing learners to authentic language use, accent variations, and cultural nuances.

Furthermore, captioning and subtitling are invaluable resources for individuals with hearing impairments, ensuring equal access to language learning opportunities. By providing inclusive captioning and subtitling options, we empower individuals from the deaf community to engage in language acquisition on an equal footing with their hearing peers.

In conclusion, captioning and subtitling have emerged as powerful tools in the realm of language acquisition. They are not only beneficial for individuals with hearing impairments but also for anyone seeking to learn a new language. By providing visual reinforcement, fostering listening skills, promoting language immersion, and ensuring inclusivity, captioning and subtitling contribute to a more effective and accessible language acquisition experience for everyone.

Chapter 6: Bilingual Education and Language Acquisition

Bilingualism and Biculturalism in Deaf Education

In the field of deaf education, the concepts of bilingualism and biculturalism play a crucial role in empowering individuals within the deaf community. Recognizing and embracing these principles not only enhance language acquisition but also foster a deeper understanding and appreciation of the diverse cultures that coexist within the deaf community.

Bilingualism, in the context of deaf education, refers to the development and use of two languages – sign language and the written/spoken language of the dominant hearing community. The use of sign language, such as American Sign Language (ASL), is integral to deaf individuals' communication and language acquisition process. ASL, being a visual-gestural language, offers a unique and expressive form of communication that allows deaf individuals to fully engage in society.

Simultaneously, the acquisition of the written and spoken language used by the dominant hearing community is equally essential. This bilingual approach provides deaf individuals with the tools necessary to interact with both deaf and hearing individuals, enabling them to navigate various social, educational, and professional environments seamlessly.

Alongside bilingualism, biculturalism is another critical aspect of deaf education. Biculturalism emphasizes the importance of understanding and embracing the cultural identity of the deaf community while simultaneously participating in the broader hearing society. By promoting biculturalism, individuals within the deaf community can maintain a strong sense of identity and pride in their cultural heritage while also being able to adapt and integrate into the larger world.

Deaf individuals who are bilingual and bicultural are more likely to experience higher levels of self-esteem, improved cognitive development, and enhanced overall academic performance. Moreover, they are better equipped to advocate for their rights and participate actively in all aspects of society.

Educators and professionals in the field of language acquisition must recognize the value of bilingualism and biculturalism in deaf education. They should prioritize the teaching of sign language alongside the dominant spoken and written language, ensuring equal access to communication and fostering inclusive learning environments.

In conclusion, embracing bilingualism and biculturalism in deaf education is vital for empowering individuals within the deaf community. By valuing and promoting sign language alongside the dominant spoken and written language, we can create a more inclusive and equitable society for all. Through this approach, we can empower deaf individuals to find their voices, celebrate their cultural heritage, and participate fully in the diverse world of language acquisition.

Benefits of Bilingual Education

In today's increasingly interconnected world, language acquisition is a vital skill that opens up a world of opportunities. The benefits of bilingual education are manifold, not only for individuals but also for society as a whole. This subchapter will explore the numerous advantages of embracing bilingual education, highlighting its positive impact on language acquisition and the wider community.

First and foremost, bilingual education enhances cognitive abilities. Research has consistently shown that bilingual individuals tend to have better problem-solving skills, enhanced creativity, and improved memory. The constant switching between languages stimulates the brain, resulting in increased mental flexibility and a greater capacity for learning. Bilingual education fosters critical thinking and problem-solving skills, enabling individuals to approach challenges from multiple perspectives.

Moreover, bilingual education promotes cultural understanding and empathy. By learning a second language, individuals gain insight into different cultures, traditions, and ways of thinking. This not only broadens their worldview but also enhances their ability to communicate and connect with people from diverse backgrounds. Bilingual education encourages tolerance, respect, and appreciation for different cultures, fostering a more harmonious and inclusive society.

Additionally, bilingual education provides a competitive edge in the global job market. In today's increasingly globalized economy, employers value individuals who possess strong language skills and cultural competence. Bilingual individuals have a broader range of job opportunities, as they can communicate with a wider range of clients, customers, and colleagues. Moreover, research has shown that bilingual employees often have higher earning potential and greater career advancement opportunities.

Furthermore, bilingual education offers unique opportunities for the deaf community. By learning sign language alongside a spoken language, individuals can bridge the communication gap between the deaf and hearing communities. This not only enhances communication and inclusivity but also paves the way for greater integration and equal opportunities for the deaf community.

In conclusion, bilingual education provides numerous benefits for individuals and society at large. From enhancing cognitive abilities and fostering cultural understanding to improving job prospects and promoting inclusivity for the deaf community, the advantages of bilingual education are undeniable. By embracing bilingual education, individuals can empower themselves and contribute to a more connected and inclusive world.

Implementing Bilingual Education Programs

Bilingual education programs have gained significant attention in recent years due to their potential to empower individuals by facilitating language acquisition in a more inclusive manner. This subchapter explores the importance of implementing bilingual education programs, particularly in the context of language acquisition for everyone, including the deaf community.

Language Acquisition for Everyone

Language acquisition is a fundamental aspect of human development, enabling individuals to communicate and connect with others. However, traditional education systems have often overlooked the diverse needs and abilities of learners, particularly those from marginalized communities, such as the deaf community. This subchapter aims to address this gap by highlighting the benefits of bilingual education programs.

Benefits of Bilingual Education

Bilingual education programs offer numerous advantages for language acquisition. By providing instruction in both the native language and a second language, these programs promote bilingualism and biliteracy, enhancing cognitive abilities and overall academic performance. Research has shown that bilingual individuals tend to have better problem-solving skills, increased creativity, and improved memory retention.

In the context of language acquisition for the deaf community, bilingual education programs play a crucial role in providing equitable opportunities for learning. These programs recognize sign language as a distinct and valid language, alongside spoken languages. By embracing sign language as an essential part of the curriculum, deaf individuals can fully develop their linguistic abilities, fostering a sense of belonging and identity within the deaf community.

Implementing Bilingual Education Programs

To effectively implement bilingual education programs, it is essential to consider several key factors. Firstly, collaboration among educators, administrators, and communities is vital to ensure inclusive and culturally sensitive instruction. This collaboration should involve deaf individuals and their families, as they possess valuable insights into the unique needs of the deaf community.

Additionally, training and professional development for educators are crucial for the successful implementation of bilingual education programs. Educators need to be knowledgeable about bilingual language acquisition strategies, including the best practices for teaching both spoken and sign languages. This expertise will enable them to create an inclusive and supportive learning environment that caters to the needs of all learners.

Conclusion

In conclusion, implementing bilingual education programs is crucial for empowering individuals and promoting language acquisition for everyone, including the deaf community. These programs offer numerous benefits, including enhanced cognitive abilities, improved academic performance, and increased cultural sensitivity. By recognizing the importance of sign language and embracing it as part of the curriculum, bilingual education programs can provide equitable opportunities for learning and foster a sense of belonging for all learners. Through collaboration and professional development, educators can effectively implement these programs and create an inclusive learning environment that celebrates language diversity.

Chapter 7: Empowering Voices: Inclusive Language Acquisition Programs

Inclusive Classrooms for Language Acquisition

In today's diverse and interconnected world, the importance of inclusive classrooms for language acquisition cannot be overstated. Language acquisition is not limited to a specific group or community; it is a fundamental skill that everyone, including the deaf community, should have access to. In this subchapter, we will explore the significance of inclusive classrooms and the benefits they bring to language acquisition.

An inclusive classroom is one that embraces diversity and provides equal opportunities for learning to all students, regardless of their linguistic or cultural backgrounds. By creating an inclusive environment, educators can foster a sense of belonging and promote the acquisition of language skills for everyone. This is particularly important for individuals from the deaf community, who may face unique challenges in language acquisition due to their reliance on sign language.

One of the key advantages of inclusive classrooms for language acquisition is the opportunity for peer learning. When students from different linguistic backgrounds come together, they can learn from each other's experiences and perspectives. This not only enhances their language skills but also promotes empathy and understanding among diverse groups of learners.

Inclusive classrooms also allow for a variety of teaching methods and accommodations to meet the needs of different learners. For example, in a class that includes deaf students, educators can incorporate visual aids, such as videos or diagrams, to ensure effective communication. Additionally, the use of sign language interpreters or captioning services can bridge the gap between deaf and hearing students, facilitating a seamless exchange of ideas and knowledge.

Moreover, inclusive classrooms promote an inclusive mindset among all students. By engaging with individuals from diverse linguistic backgrounds, students develop a greater appreciation for cultural diversity and learn to value different languages and communication styles. This not only prepares them for a globalized world but also nurtures a sense of respect and inclusivity that extends beyond the classroom.

In conclusion, inclusive classrooms play a vital role in language acquisition for everyone, including the deaf community. They provide a platform for peer learning, enable the use of diverse teaching methods, and foster an inclusive mindset among students. By embracing diversity and ensuring equal access to language acquisition, inclusive classrooms empower learners to become effective communicators and active participants in an increasingly interconnected world.

Collaborative Approaches in Language Acquisition Programs

Language acquisition is a complex process that requires a comprehensive and collaborative approach. In today's diverse society, it is crucial to develop language acquisition programs that cater to the needs of everyone, including the deaf community. This subchapter explores the importance of collaborative approaches in language acquisition programs and how they can empower voices and promote inclusive communication.

Collaboration is key in language acquisition programs as it brings together various stakeholders, including educators, parents, language experts, and community members. By working together, they can create an environment that fosters effective language learning and enables individuals to communicate with confidence and fluency. Collaborative approaches ensure that language acquisition programs are inclusive and consider the unique needs and perspectives of different individuals.

One of the fundamental aspects of collaborative approaches in language acquisition programs is the involvement of the deaf community. Deaf individuals have their own distinct language, such as sign language, which is essential for their communication. By engaging the deaf community in the design and implementation of language acquisition programs, their expertise and experiences can be leveraged to create more effective learning strategies. This collaboration also promotes a sense of belonging and empowerment among the deaf community, ensuring that their voices are heard and valued.

Collaborative approaches also emphasize the importance of involving parents and caregivers in language acquisition programs. Parents play a vital role in a child's language development, and their active participation can significantly impact the child's progress. By providing parents with resources, support, and training, language acquisition programs can empower them to create language-rich environments at home. This collaboration between educators, parents, and caregivers helps ensure consistency in language learning and fosters a strong foundation for future language acquisition.

Furthermore, collaborative approaches encourage partnerships between schools, organizations, and community members. Language acquisition programs can benefit from community involvement by incorporating real-life scenarios and cultural experiences into the learning process. This collaboration broadens students' understanding of language and promotes cultural diversity and inclusion.

In conclusion, collaborative approaches are essential in language acquisition programs for everyone, including the deaf community. By involving various stakeholders, such as educators, parents, language experts, and the community, these programs can create an inclusive and empowering environment for language learning. Collaboration ensures that the unique needs and perspectives of individuals are considered, leading to more effective language acquisition strategies. By fostering partnerships and involving the deaf community, parents, and caregivers, language acquisition programs can empower voices and promote inclusive communication for all.

Advocacy and Support for Language Acquisition in the Deaf Community

Language acquisition is a fundamental aspect of human development, allowing individuals to express their thoughts, feelings, and ideas. While language acquisition is a natural process for most people, it presents unique challenges for the deaf community. In this subchapter, we will explore the importance of advocacy and support for language acquisition in the deaf community, with a focus on inclusive practices that benefit everyone.

The deaf community comprises individuals who use sign language as their primary means of communication. For these individuals, acquiring language skills is crucial for their personal, social, and educational development. However, due to various factors such as limited access to linguistic input and inadequate support systems, many individuals in the deaf community face significant barriers to language acquisition.

Advocacy plays a pivotal role in addressing these challenges and creating an inclusive environment for language acquisition. By advocating for accessible education, sign language recognition, and inclusive policies, we can ensure that individuals in the deaf community have equal opportunities to acquire language skills. This involves raising awareness among policymakers, educators, and the general public about the needs and rights of the deaf community.

Support for language acquisition in the deaf community can take various forms. For instance, implementing bilingual education programs that incorporate both sign language and written/oral language can enhance language development for deaf individuals. Additionally, providing access to qualified sign language interpreters and speech therapists can facilitate effective communication and promote language acquisition.

Moreover, technology has played a crucial role in empowering the deaf community. Advancements such as captioning services, video relay services, and mobile applications have significantly improved access to communication and language learning resources. By promoting the use of these technologies and ensuring their availability, we can further support language acquisition in the deaf community.

In conclusion, advocating for and providing support for language acquisition in the deaf community is essential for fostering inclusive practices and empowering individuals. By recognizing the unique needs of the deaf community and implementing inclusive policies, we can create an environment where language acquisition is accessible to all. Whether you are an educator, policymaker, or a member of society, it is crucial to understand the importance of language acquisition for everyone, including the deaf community, and actively contribute to their empowerment.

Chapter 8: Enhancing Language Acquisition through Multimodal Approaches

Visual and Tactile Modalities in Language Acquisition

Language acquisition is a fascinating process that allows individuals to communicate, express emotions, and connect with others. While spoken language is the most common form of communication, it is essential to acknowledge that not everyone acquires language through auditory means. In fact, visual and tactile modalities play a crucial role in language acquisition for many individuals, including those in the deaf community.

Visual modalities refer to the use of visual cues, such as sign language or lip-reading, to comprehend and express language. Sign language is a rich and complex visual-gestural system that relies on handshapes, facial expressions, and body movements to convey meaning. For deaf individuals, sign language is their primary language, and it provides them with a foundation for communication, social interaction, and cognitive development. By recognizing the importance of visual modalities, we can empower individuals in the deaf community to fully participate in society, education, and various aspects of life.

Tactile modalities involve the sense of touch and play a significant role in language acquisition for individuals who are both deaf and blind. These individuals rely on tactile sign language, which involves the use of touch to feel and interpret sign language. Through tactile signing, deaf-blind individuals can feel the movements and handshapes made by the signer, allowing them to understand and express language effectively. This modality fosters a unique form of communication and connection, highlighting the diverse ways in which language can be acquired and expressed.

Understanding and embracing visual and tactile modalities in language acquisition is not only crucial for individuals within the deaf and deaf-blind communities but for everyone. By recognizing the different modalities through which people acquire language, we can create inclusive environments that cater to the diverse needs of individuals. This inclusivity extends beyond language acquisition and promotes a more inclusive society overall.

Educational institutions, workplaces, and public spaces should strive to become more accessible by incorporating visual and tactile modalities into their communication strategies. This can involve providing sign language interpreters, offering tactile signing resources, or implementing technologies that aid in visual communication. By doing so, we empower individuals to express themselves fully and participate actively in various aspects of life.

In conclusion, visual and tactile modalities are vital components in language acquisition, particularly for individuals in the deaf and deaf-blind communities. By acknowledging and embracing these modalities, we can create a more inclusive and accessible society where everyone, regardless of their hearing abilities, can communicate and connect effectively. Let us empower voices through language acquisition, ensuring that no one is left behind.

Multimodal Learning Strategies

In today's diverse and interconnected world, language acquisition has become more important than ever. Whether you are a parent, a teacher, a student, or simply someone interested in learning a new language, understanding the various strategies for effective language acquisition is crucial. One such strategy that has gained significant attention is multimodal learning.

Multimodal learning refers to the use of multiple sensory channels, such as visual, auditory, and kinesthetic, to enhance the learning experience. This approach recognizes that individuals have different learning styles and preferences, and by incorporating various modalities, we can optimize language acquisition for everyone, including the deaf community.

Visual aids, such as pictures, videos, and gestures, play a vital role in multimodal learning. These visual cues provide context, support understanding, and reinforce linguistic concepts. For instance, when learning new vocabulary, associating words with corresponding images can help create a mental connection, facilitating retention. Additionally, using sign language or other visual communication methods can greatly benefit the deaf community, allowing them to engage in language acquisition on equal footing with their hearing counterparts.

Auditory components, such as listening to native speakers, recordings, or podcasts, are also essential in multimodal learning. By exposing oneself to authentic language input, learners can develop their listening skills, improve pronunciation, and gain a deeper understanding of intonation and rhythm. This is particularly valuable for those who aim to become fluent speakers or communicate effectively with others in real-life situations.

Kinesthetic activities, involving physical movement and tactile experiences, are another valuable aspect of multimodal learning. Role-playing, interactive games, and hands-on exercises help reinforce language concepts and make learning more engaging and memorable. Furthermore, incorporating physical gestures while speaking or signing can enhance communication and aid in language comprehension, making it an inclusive strategy for both hearing and deaf individuals.

By embracing multimodal learning strategies, we can empower individuals of all backgrounds and abilities to acquire language effectively. This approach not only caters to different learning styles but also promotes inclusivity and diversity in language acquisition. Whether you are a visual learner, an auditory learner, or prefer a more hands-on approach, multimodal learning offers a versatile toolkit to support your language learning journey.

In conclusion, the incorporation of multimodal learning strategies is vital for language acquisition in today's world. By utilizing visual, auditory, and kinesthetic modalities, we can create a comprehensive learning experience that benefits everyone, including the deaf community. Whether you are a language teacher, a parent, or a language learner yourself, understanding and implementing these strategies will undoubtedly enhance the language acquisition process and empower voices from all walks of life.

Chapter 9: Promoting Language Acquisition in Everyday Settings

Language Acquisition at Home

Language acquisition is a fascinating and essential process that occurs naturally in every human being. It is through language that we communicate, express our thoughts and emotions, and connect with others. While language acquisition may seem effortless for many, it is important to understand that it is a complex process that requires a nurturing environment. In this subchapter, we will explore the significance of language acquisition at home and how it can empower individuals, including those in the deaf community.

At home, language acquisition begins from the moment a child is born. It is within the family unit that children first learn to communicate and develop their linguistic abilities. Parents and caregivers play a crucial role in creating a rich language environment that fosters language acquisition. By engaging in conversations, reading books, singing songs, and providing language-rich experiences, parents can help their children build a strong foundation in language.

For individuals in the deaf community, language acquisition at home takes on a unique dimension. American Sign Language (ASL) is the primary language for many deaf individuals, and it is crucial for them to have access to ASL from an early age. Just as hearing children benefit from exposure to spoken language, deaf children thrive when they have access to fluent sign language users.

In an inclusive society, it is essential to recognize that language acquisition is not limited to spoken languages alone. Sign languages, such as ASL, are fully-fledged languages with their own grammatical rules and cultural expressions. By embracing and supporting sign language acquisition, we empower the deaf community to fully participate in all aspects of life.

Language acquisition at home is not limited to childhood. It is a lifelong journey that continues to evolve and adapt. In today's interconnected world, individuals have the opportunity to learn and acquire multiple languages, expanding their cultural horizons and fostering global understanding.

In conclusion, language acquisition at home is a powerful tool that empowers individuals, including those in the deaf community. By creating a nurturing language environment, we can support the development of strong linguistic skills and promote inclusivity. Whether it is through spoken languages or sign languages, language acquisition enables us to connect, express ourselves, and understand the world around us. Let us embrace the diversity of languages and empower voices from all walks of life.

Language Acquisition in Community Settings

In any society, language acquisition plays a vital role in communication and social interaction. It is a fundamental process that allows individuals to express their thoughts, emotions, and ideas, and to connect with others on a deep level. While language acquisition can occur through various means, community settings have proven to be particularly powerful and effective environments for learning and enhancing language skills.

Community settings provide individuals with a rich linguistic environment where they can engage in meaningful interactions with others who share a common language. These settings offer ample opportunities for language learners to practice and refine their language skills, as well as to gain a deeper understanding of cultural nuances and social norms associated with the language.

One of the key advantages of language acquisition in community settings is the exposure to native speakers. Interacting with native speakers allows learners to grasp the subtleties of pronunciation, intonation, and idiomatic expressions that are often difficult to acquire solely through classroom instruction. Through continuous exposure and practice, learners gradually develop fluency and confidence in their language skills.

Furthermore, community settings foster a sense of belonging and create a supportive environment for language learners. Being part of a community of language speakers enables individuals to engage in authentic conversations, exchanging ideas and experiences while receiving constructive feedback. This collaborative learning approach not only accelerates language acquisition but also promotes cultural understanding and empathy.

Language acquisition in community settings is particularly relevant to the Deaf community. For individuals who are deaf or hard of hearing, community settings play a crucial role in acquiring sign language skills. Deaf individuals rely heavily on visual communication, and being part of a community that uses sign language allows them to fully immerse themselves in the language and gain fluency.

In conclusion, language acquisition in community settings offers numerous benefits for learners of all backgrounds. The exposure to native speakers, the opportunity for authentic conversations, and the sense of belonging all contribute to a holistic and effective language learning experience. Whether it is learning a spoken language or sign language, community settings provide an ideal platform for individuals to acquire and enhance their language skills. By embracing the power of community settings, we can empower voices and ensure that language acquisition is accessible and inclusive for everyone.

Language Acquisition in Educational Institutions

In today's globalized world, language acquisition plays a crucial role in empowering individuals to effectively communicate and engage with the diverse communities around them. Educational institutions play a vital role in facilitating this process, offering comprehensive language acquisition programs that cater to the needs of every individual, including those in the deaf community. This subchapter explores the importance of language acquisition in educational institutions and its impact on empowering voices.

Educational institutions serve as a nurturing ground for language acquisition, providing a structured and conducive environment for individuals to learn and master various languages. Language acquisition programs in schools, colleges, and universities aim to equip students with the necessary linguistic skills to communicate, understand, and express their thoughts effectively. These programs not only focus on the spoken language but also recognize the importance of sign languages, such as American Sign Language (ASL), in empowering individuals from the deaf community.

Language acquisition in educational institutions fosters inclusivity and promotes a sense of belonging among students from diverse linguistic backgrounds. It allows individuals to appreciate and respect different cultures and languages, enabling them to become global citizens who can effectively participate in the interconnected world. Furthermore, language acquisition programs equip individuals with the tools to break down communication barriers and promote understanding and empathy among different communities.

For the deaf community, language acquisition programs in educational institutions play a pivotal role in bridging the communication gap between deaf and hearing individuals. By offering comprehensive sign language courses, these institutions empower deaf individuals to express themselves freely and participate fully in the educational setting. Additionally, these programs create awareness and understanding among hearing individuals, fostering a more inclusive and accessible environment for everyone.

Language acquisition in educational institutions not only focuses on acquiring language skills but also emphasizes the importance of cultural competence. By immersing students in different cultures and languages, these programs enable individuals to appreciate and embrace diversity, promoting a more inclusive and tolerant society.

In conclusion, language acquisition in educational institutions is vital for empowering voices and creating a more inclusive society. By offering comprehensive language programs that cater to the needs of every individual, including the deaf community, educational institutions play a crucial role in equipping individuals with the linguistic skills and cultural competence necessary to participate actively in today's globalized world. Language acquisition programs foster understanding, empathy, and inclusivity, enabling individuals to communicate effectively and engage meaningfully with diverse communities around them.

Chapter 10: Future Directions in Language Acquisition for the Deaf Community

Advancements in Language Acquisition Research

Language acquisition is a fascinating field that has seen significant advancements in recent years. Researchers from various disciplines have dedicated their efforts to understanding how individuals acquire and process language, leading to breakthroughs that have empowered people from all walks of life, including the deaf community. This subchapter explores some of the most noteworthy advancements in language acquisition research and their implications for everyone.

One groundbreaking area of research is the study of critical periods in language acquisition. Historically, it was believed that there was a window of opportunity during childhood when language could be acquired effortlessly. However, recent studies have challenged this notion, suggesting that language acquisition can occur at any age. This discovery has given hope to individuals who may have missed out on language development during their early years, such as those who are deaf or have hearing impairments.

Another significant advancement is the exploration of different language acquisition methodologies. Traditional approaches have primarily focused on spoken languages, leaving those with hearing disabilities at a disadvantage. However, researchers have now developed innovative techniques that cater specifically to the needs of the deaf community. These methods incorporate visual and tactile cues, making language acquisition more accessible and inclusive for everyone.

Advancements in technology have also revolutionized language acquisition. Augmented reality, virtual reality, and mobile applications have become powerful tools in language learning. These technologies offer immersive experiences, allowing learners to practice their language skills in real-world scenarios. Additionally, online platforms and language learning apps provide personalized and adaptive learning experiences, catering to the diverse needs of language learners.

Neuroscientific research has provided valuable insights into the brain mechanisms underlying language acquisition. By studying brain activity using techniques like functional magnetic resonance imaging (fMRI), researchers have discovered the neural pathways associated with language processing. This knowledge has paved the way for targeted interventions, such as neurofeedback training, which can enhance language acquisition for individuals with language difficulties.

In conclusion, the field of language acquisition research has made remarkable strides in recent years. These advancements have not only benefited the general population but have also empowered the deaf community and others with language-related challenges. By understanding the critical periods of language acquisition, developing inclusive methodologies, leveraging technology, and exploring the neural basis of language processing, language acquisition has become more accessible, effective, and enjoyable for everyone. This subchapter aims to shed light on these advancements, encouraging readers to embrace the possibilities and opportunities that arise from a deeper understanding of language acquisition.

Inclusive Language Acquisition Policies

In the diverse world we live in today, it is crucial to ensure that everyone has access to language acquisition opportunities. Language acquisition is not only important for communication, but it also plays a significant role in fostering social integration, personal development, and educational advancement. However, there are many barriers that prevent certain individuals, including members of the deaf community, from fully participating in language acquisition programs. In this subchapter, we will explore the concept of inclusive language acquisition policies and their importance in creating an equal and accessible learning environment for everyone.

Inclusive language acquisition policies aim to remove the barriers that prevent individuals from acquiring language skills. These policies focus on providing equal opportunities for individuals of all backgrounds, abilities, and communication preferences. By implementing inclusive policies, we can ensure that language acquisition programs cater to the diverse needs and learning styles of every individual.

One key aspect of inclusive language acquisition policies is the recognition and inclusion of the deaf community. Sign languages are complete and natural languages with their own grammar and syntax. Therefore, it is essential to facilitate sign language acquisition alongside spoken language acquisition. Inclusive language acquisition policies should prioritize the provision of sign language interpreters, captioning, and other assistive technologies to ensure effective communication for deaf individuals.

Additionally, inclusive language acquisition policies should address the needs of individuals with other communication preferences, such as those who use augmentative and alternative communication (AAC) devices. These policies should ensure that AAC users have access to the necessary technologies and support to facilitate their language acquisition journey.

Furthermore, inclusive language acquisition policies should promote cultural sensitivity and respect for all language communities. This includes acknowledging and valuing the different languages and dialects spoken within a society, as well as encouraging the preservation and revitalization of endangered languages.

By implementing inclusive language acquisition policies, we can empower individuals from all backgrounds to develop their linguistic skills and fully participate in society. Language acquisition is a fundamental right, and it is our responsibility to ensure that everyone, regardless of their abilities or communication preferences, has equal access to language learning opportunities.

In conclusion, inclusive language acquisition policies are essential for creating an equitable and accessible learning environment for everyone. These policies should prioritize the inclusion of the deaf community, individuals with different communication preferences, and promote cultural sensitivity. By embracing inclusivity in language acquisition, we can empower voices, promote social integration, and foster personal and educational growth for individuals of all backgrounds.

Empowering the Deaf Community through Language Acquisition

Language is the key to communication, connection, and understanding. It shapes our thoughts, influences our interactions, and enables us to express our ideas and emotions. However, for the deaf community, language acquisition can be a unique and challenging journey. In this subchapter, we explore the importance of empowering the deaf community through language acquisition, ensuring equal opportunities for communication, education, and integration.

Language acquisition is a fundamental human right, and it is essential that every individual, including the deaf community, has access to effective language learning methods. For years, sign language has been the primary means of communication for many deaf individuals, serving as their native language. However, it is crucial to recognize that sign language is not universal and may vary across different regions and cultures. Therefore, it is essential to provide resources and support for deaf individuals to learn and acquire sign language specific to their community.

In recent years, advancements in technology and educational approaches have significantly contributed to empowering the deaf community in language acquisition. The introduction of assistive devices, such as cochlear implants and hearing aids, has opened up new avenues for deaf individuals to learn spoken languages. These devices help bridge the gap between the hearing and deaf worlds, allowing for enhanced communication and language development.

Furthermore, educational institutions and organizations have recognized the importance of providing inclusive and accessible education for the deaf community. Specialized schools and programs focusing on sign language education have emerged, ensuring that deaf individuals have the opportunity to acquire language skills and interact with peers who share similar experiences. Additionally, educators and professionals are being trained in deaf culture and sign language interpretation, enabling them to effectively communicate and support the deaf community's language acquisition journey.

Language acquisition for the deaf community goes beyond the acquisition of sign language or spoken languages. It also encompasses the development of written language skills and literacy. Accessible materials, such as books, online resources, and captioned videos, are vital in facilitating language acquisition and promoting inclusivity.

By empowering the deaf community through language acquisition, we enable them to participate fully in society, access education and employment opportunities, and express their thoughts and emotions freely. It is crucial for individuals, educational institutions, and policymakers to work together to ensure equal access to language learning resources and support for the deaf community. Through this collective effort, we can create a more inclusive and diverse society that values and embraces the linguistic diversity of every individual, including the deaf community.

Conclusion: Empowering Voices: Language Acquisition for Everyone, Including the Deaf Community

In this book, "Empowering Voices: Language Acquisition for Everyone, Including the Deaf Community," we have explored the importance of language acquisition for individuals from all walks of life, with a particular focus on the deaf community. Language is a fundamental human right, and it is crucial for us to create inclusive environments that empower everyone to express themselves and be understood.

Throughout the chapters, we have discussed various aspects of language acquisition, including the different methods and techniques that can be employed to facilitate effective communication. We have delved into the challenges faced by the deaf community in acquiring language, and we have highlighted the significance of sign languages as a means of expression and connection.

Language acquisition is not limited to spoken languages alone; it extends to sign languages as well. Many misconceptions exist surrounding sign languages, often leading to their marginalization. However, we have emphasized that sign languages are complete and complex systems of communication, with their own grammatical structures and cultural nuances. It is vital to acknowledge and celebrate the richness of sign languages, ensuring that they are recognized as legitimate languages in their own right.

In our exploration of language acquisition for the deaf community, we have also emphasized the importance of early intervention and access to education. Early exposure to sign language, along with appropriate educational support, can significantly enhance language development and social integration for individuals who are deaf. It is crucial for educational institutions and society at large to provide the necessary resources and accommodations to enable the successful acquisition of language for everyone.

Language acquisition is not solely the responsibility of the individual; it is a collective effort that requires the active participation of communities, educators, and policymakers. By fostering inclusive environments that value and support language diversity, we can empower voices and create a more inclusive society for everyone, including the deaf community. Everyone deserves the opportunity to express themselves, be understood, and participate fully in the social, cultural, and economic aspects of life.

As we conclude our journey through "Empowering Voices: Language Acquisition for Everyone, Including the Deaf Community," let us remember that language is a powerful tool that connects us all. By embracing and supporting language acquisition for everyone, we can foster understanding, empathy, and equality, ultimately creating a more inclusive and harmonious world. Let us work together to empower voices and ensure that language acquisition is accessible to all, regardless of their abilities or backgrounds.

www.ingramcontent.com/pod-product-compliance
Lightning Source LLC
Chambersburg PA
CBHW070320160726
47999CB00003B/1087